50 Premium Ocean Dishes

By: Kelly Johnson

Table of Contents

- Lobster Thermidor
- Grilled Chilean Sea Bass with Lemon Butter
- Seared Scallops with Truffle Cream Sauce
- King Crab Legs with Garlic Butter
- Oysters Rockefeller
- Pan-Seared Halibut with White Wine Sauce
- Saffron-Infused Seafood Paella
- Butter-Poached Lobster Tail
- Miso-Glazed Black Cod
- Bluefin Tuna Tartare
- Charcoal-Grilled Octopus with Citrus Dressing
- Alaskan King Salmon with Maple Glaze
- Swordfish Steak with Chimichurri
- Wild-Caught Red Snapper in Coconut Curry
- Dover Sole Meunière
- Bouillabaisse (French Seafood Stew)
- Caviar-Topped Smoked Salmon Blinis
- Langoustine with Garlic and Lemon
- Shrimp Scampi with White Wine Sauce
- Atlantic Cod with Saffron Risotto
- Crab-Stuffed Flounder
- Sushi-Grade Ahi Tuna Poke Bowl
- Caribbean Grilled Mahi-Mahi
- Whole Roasted Branzino with Herbs
- Steamed Clams with Chardonnay Butter
- Seafood Cioppino
- Lobster Mac and Cheese
- Thai Spicy Prawn Tom Yum Soup
- Truffle-Infused Lobster Risotto
- Charred Mackerel with Pickled Vegetables
- Fried Soft-Shell Crab with Remoulade
- Szechuan-Style Spicy Lobster
- Butter-Basted Grouper Fillet
- Scallop and Saffron Cream Pasta
- Smoked Haddock Chowder

- Cured Gravlax with Dill Mustard Sauce
- Spanish Gambas al Ajillo (Garlic Shrimp)
- Teriyaki-Glazed Yellowtail
- Baked Clams Casino
- Japanese Uni (Sea Urchin) Sashimi
- Mediterranean Stuffed Squid
- Cajun Blackened Redfish
- New England Lobster Roll
- Hokkaido Scallop Carpaccio
- Icelandic Salted Cod with Potatoes
- Sicilian-Style Grilled Sardines
- Alaskan Spot Prawns with Garlic Butter
- Poached Monkfish in Saffron Broth
- Seaweed-Wrapped Grilled Eel (Unagi)
- Italian Frutti di Mare (Seafood Pasta)

Lobster Thermidor

Ingredients:

- 2 lobster tails
- 2 tbsp butter
- 1 shallot, minced
- 2 tbsp flour
- 1/2 cup white wine
- 1/2 cup heavy cream
- 1 tbsp Dijon mustard
- 1/4 cup Parmesan cheese, grated
- 1 egg yolk
- Salt & pepper
- Paprika for garnish

Instructions:

1. Cook lobster tails, remove meat, and chop.
2. Sauté shallot in butter, add flour, cook for 1 minute.
3. Stir in wine, cream, mustard, and cheese until thickened.
4. Remove from heat, stir in yolk, add lobster meat.
5. Stuff shells, sprinkle with paprika, and broil until golden.

Grilled Chilean Sea Bass with Lemon Butter

Ingredients:

- 2 Chilean sea bass fillets
- 2 tbsp olive oil
- 2 tbsp butter
- 1 lemon, juiced
- 1 garlic clove, minced
- Salt & pepper
- Fresh parsley for garnish

Instructions:

1. Preheat grill and brush fish with olive oil.
2. Grill for 4-5 minutes per side.
3. Melt butter, stir in lemon juice and garlic.
4. Drizzle over fish, garnish with parsley.

Seared Scallops with Truffle Cream Sauce

Ingredients:

- 8 large scallops
- 2 tbsp butter
- 1/2 cup heavy cream
- 1 tsp truffle oil
- 1 garlic clove, minced
- Salt & pepper
- Chives for garnish

Instructions:

1. Sear scallops in butter for 2 minutes per side. Remove.
2. Sauté garlic, add cream, and simmer.
3. Stir in truffle oil, season with salt and pepper.
4. Return scallops, coat in sauce, and garnish with chives.

King Crab Legs with Garlic Butter

Ingredients:

- 2 lbs king crab legs
- 1/2 cup butter
- 3 garlic cloves, minced
- 1 lemon, juiced
- 1 tsp paprika
- Salt & pepper

Instructions:

1. Steam crab legs for 5 minutes.
2. Melt butter, sauté garlic, stir in lemon juice and paprika.
3. Serve crab legs with garlic butter.

Oysters Rockefeller

Ingredients:

- 12 fresh oysters
- 2 tbsp butter
- 1 shallot, minced
- 1 cup spinach, chopped
- 1/4 cup Parmesan cheese
- 1/4 cup breadcrumbs
- 2 tbsp Pernod (or white wine)
- Salt & pepper
- Lemon wedges for serving

Instructions:

1. Preheat oven to 400°F (200°C).
2. Sauté shallot in butter, add spinach, Pernod, and season.
3. Top oysters with mixture, sprinkle with cheese and breadcrumbs.
4. Bake for 10 minutes until golden.

Pan-Seared Halibut with White Wine Sauce

Ingredients:

- 2 halibut fillets
- 2 tbsp butter
- 1/2 cup white wine
- 1 shallot, minced
- 1/4 cup heavy cream
- Salt & pepper
- Fresh dill for garnish

Instructions:

1. Sear halibut in butter for 3-4 minutes per side. Remove.
2. Sauté shallot, deglaze with wine, simmer.
3. Stir in cream, season, and pour over halibut.
4. Garnish with dill.

Saffron-Infused Seafood Paella

Ingredients:

- 1 cup Arborio rice
- 2 cups seafood broth
- 1/4 tsp saffron
- 1/2 lb shrimp
- 1/2 lb mussels
- 1/2 lb calamari rings
- 1 onion, chopped
- 2 garlic cloves, minced
- 1 bell pepper, sliced
- 1 tomato, diced
- 1 tsp smoked paprika
- 2 tbsp olive oil

Instructions:

1. Sauté onion, garlic, and bell pepper in olive oil.
2. Add rice, saffron, tomatoes, and paprika.
3. Stir in broth, simmer until rice is tender.
4. Add seafood, cook for 5 minutes.

Butter-Poached Lobster Tail

Ingredients:

- 2 lobster tails
- 1/2 cup butter
- 1 garlic clove, minced
- 1 tbsp lemon juice
- Salt & pepper

Instructions:

1. Melt butter with garlic and lemon juice.
2. Add lobster tails and poach for 5 minutes.
3. Serve with extra butter sauce.

Miso-Glazed Black Cod

Ingredients:

- 2 black cod fillets
- 2 tbsp white miso paste
- 2 tbsp mirin
- 1 tbsp soy sauce
- 1 tbsp sake
- 1 tbsp honey

Instructions:

1. Mix miso, mirin, soy sauce, sake, and honey.
2. Marinate cod for 2 hours.
3. Broil for 8-10 minutes.

Bluefin Tuna Tartare

Ingredients:

- 6 oz sushi-grade bluefin tuna, finely diced
- 1 tbsp soy sauce
- 1 tsp sesame oil
- 1 tsp lime juice
- 1/2 tsp grated ginger
- 1 tbsp finely chopped scallions
- 1 tsp black sesame seeds
- 1/2 avocado, diced
- Microgreens for garnish

Instructions:

1. In a bowl, mix tuna, soy sauce, sesame oil, lime juice, ginger, and scallions.
2. Gently fold in diced avocado.
3. Garnish with sesame seeds and microgreens.
4. Serve chilled with crackers or crispy wontons.

Charcoal-Grilled Octopus with Citrus Dressing

Ingredients:

- 1 whole octopus (about 2 lbs), cleaned
- 2 tbsp olive oil
- 1 lemon, juiced
- 1 orange, juiced
- 1 tsp smoked paprika
- 2 garlic cloves, minced
- Salt & pepper
- Fresh parsley for garnish

Instructions:

1. Simmer octopus in salted water for 45 minutes until tender.
2. Drain, let cool, and cut into sections.
3. Brush with olive oil, season with salt, pepper, and paprika.
4. Grill over charcoal for 2-3 minutes per side.
5. Drizzle with citrus dressing and garnish with parsley.

Alaskan King Salmon with Maple Glaze

Ingredients:

- 2 salmon fillets
- 1/4 cup maple syrup
- 1 tbsp Dijon mustard
- 1 tbsp soy sauce
- 1 tsp garlic powder
- Salt & pepper

Instructions:

1. Preheat oven to 400°F (200°C).
2. Mix maple syrup, Dijon, soy sauce, and garlic powder.
3. Brush glaze over salmon.
4. Bake for 12-15 minutes.

Swordfish Steak with Chimichurri

Ingredients:

- 2 swordfish steaks
- 2 tbsp olive oil
- 1 tsp salt & pepper

For Chimichurri:

- 1/2 cup parsley, chopped
- 2 garlic cloves, minced
- 1 tbsp red wine vinegar
- 1/2 tsp red pepper flakes
- 1/4 cup olive oil

Instructions:

1. Brush swordfish with oil, salt, and pepper.
2. Grill for 3-4 minutes per side.
3. Mix chimichurri ingredients and spoon over cooked fish.

Wild-Caught Red Snapper in Coconut Curry

Ingredients:

- 2 red snapper fillets
- 1 tbsp coconut oil
- 1 onion, chopped
- 2 garlic cloves, minced
- 1-inch ginger, grated
- 1 can (14 oz) coconut milk
- 1 tbsp red curry paste
- 1 tbsp fish sauce
- Juice of 1 lime

Instructions:

1. Sauté onion, garlic, and ginger in coconut oil.
2. Stir in curry paste, coconut milk, and fish sauce. Simmer.
3. Add snapper fillets and poach for 10 minutes.
4. Finish with lime juice.

Dover Sole Meunière

Ingredients:

- 2 Dover sole fillets
- 1/4 cup flour
- 2 tbsp butter
- 1 lemon, juiced
- 1 tbsp capers
- Salt & pepper

Instructions:

1. Dredge sole in flour, season with salt and pepper.
2. Pan-fry in butter for 2-3 minutes per side.
3. Add lemon juice and capers to the pan.
4. Serve with sauce spooned over.

Bouillabaisse (French Seafood Stew)

Ingredients:

- 1 lb mixed seafood (shrimp, mussels, clams, white fish)
- 1 onion, chopped
- 3 garlic cloves, minced
- 2 tbsp olive oil
- 1 cup white wine
- 3 cups fish stock
- 1 can (14 oz) diced tomatoes
- 1/2 tsp saffron
- 1 tsp fresh thyme

Instructions:

1. Sauté onion and garlic in olive oil.
2. Add wine, stock, tomatoes, saffron, and thyme. Simmer.
3. Add seafood and cook for 5 minutes.

Caviar-Topped Smoked Salmon Blinis

Ingredients:

- 12 mini blinis (small pancakes)
- 4 oz smoked salmon
- 2 tbsp crème fraîche
- 1 oz black caviar
- Fresh dill

Instructions:

1. Top blinis with smoked salmon and crème fraîche.
2. Add a small spoonful of caviar.
3. Garnish with fresh dill.

Langoustine with Garlic and Lemon

Ingredients:

- 6 langoustines
- 2 tbsp butter
- 2 garlic cloves, minced
- 1 lemon, juiced
- Salt & pepper
- Fresh parsley

Instructions:

1. Sauté garlic in butter, add langoustines.
2. Cook for 5 minutes.
3. Squeeze over lemon juice, season, and garnish with parsley.

Shrimp Scampi with White Wine Sauce

Ingredients:

- 1/2 lb shrimp, peeled and deveined
- 2 tbsp butter
- 3 garlic cloves, minced
- 1/2 cup white wine
- 1/2 tsp red pepper flakes
- Juice of 1 lemon
- Fresh parsley

Instructions:

1. Sauté garlic in butter.
2. Add shrimp, cook for 2 minutes.
3. Pour in white wine and lemon juice, simmer.
4. Garnish with parsley.

Atlantic Cod with Saffron Risotto

Ingredients:

- 2 cod fillets
- 1 tbsp olive oil
- Salt & pepper

For Saffron Risotto:

- 1 cup Arborio rice
- 3 cups chicken or seafood broth
- 1/4 cup dry white wine
- 1/4 tsp saffron threads
- 1/2 onion, finely chopped
- 1 tbsp butter
- 1/4 cup Parmesan cheese

Instructions:

1. Heat broth and steep saffron.
2. Sauté onion in butter, add Arborio rice.
3. Stir in wine, cook until absorbed.
4. Gradually add broth, stirring until creamy.
5. Stir in Parmesan and season.
6. Sear cod fillets in olive oil for 3-4 minutes per side.
7. Serve cod over risotto.

Crab-Stuffed Flounder

Ingredients:

- 2 flounder fillets
- 1/2 cup lump crab meat
- 2 tbsp mayonnaise
- 1 tbsp Dijon mustard
- 1/4 cup breadcrumbs
- 1 tbsp chopped parsley
- 1/2 tsp Old Bay seasoning

Instructions:

1. Preheat oven to 375°F (190°C).
2. Mix crab, mayo, mustard, breadcrumbs, parsley, and Old Bay.
3. Spoon mixture onto fillets and roll up.
4. Bake for 15-18 minutes.

Sushi-Grade Ahi Tuna Poke Bowl

Ingredients:

- 6 oz sushi-grade ahi tuna, cubed
- 2 tbsp soy sauce
- 1 tsp sesame oil
- 1 tsp rice vinegar
- 1 tsp sriracha
- 1/2 avocado, diced
- 1/4 cup edamame
- 1/4 cup shredded carrots
- 1 cup sushi rice, cooked
- Sesame seeds and green onions for garnish

Instructions:

1. Mix tuna with soy sauce, sesame oil, vinegar, and sriracha.
2. Assemble rice, tuna, avocado, edamame, and carrots in a bowl.
3. Garnish with sesame seeds and green onions.

Caribbean Grilled Mahi-Mahi

Ingredients:

- 2 mahi-mahi fillets
- 2 tbsp olive oil
- 1 tsp allspice
- 1 tsp garlic powder
- 1/2 tsp cayenne
- 1 lime, juiced

Instructions:

1. Rub fillets with oil, spices, and lime juice.
2. Grill for 3-4 minutes per side.

Whole Roasted Branzino with Herbs

Ingredients:

- 1 whole branzino, cleaned
- 2 tbsp olive oil
- 2 garlic cloves, minced
- 1 lemon, sliced
- 1 tbsp fresh thyme
- 1 tbsp fresh rosemary
- Salt & pepper

Instructions:

1. Preheat oven to 400°F (200°C).
2. Stuff branzino with lemon slices and herbs.
3. Drizzle with olive oil and garlic.
4. Roast for 20-25 minutes.

Steamed Clams with Chardonnay Butter

Ingredients:

- 2 lbs littleneck clams, scrubbed
- 2 tbsp butter
- 2 garlic cloves, minced
- 1/2 cup Chardonnay
- 1 tbsp chopped parsley
- Lemon wedges

Instructions:

1. Sauté garlic in butter.
2. Add wine and clams, cover and steam until opened.
3. Garnish with parsley and lemon.

Seafood Cioppino

Ingredients:

- 1 lb mixed seafood (shrimp, mussels, clams, white fish)
- 1 onion, chopped
- 3 garlic cloves, minced
- 2 tbsp olive oil
- 1 cup white wine
- 3 cups fish stock
- 1 can (14 oz) diced tomatoes
- 1/2 tsp red pepper flakes
- 1 tsp fresh thyme

Instructions:

1. Sauté onion and garlic in olive oil.
2. Add wine, stock, tomatoes, and spices. Simmer.
3. Add seafood and cook for 5 minutes.

Lobster Mac and Cheese

Ingredients:

- 2 lobster tails, cooked and chopped
- 8 oz elbow macaroni
- 2 tbsp butter
- 2 tbsp flour
- 2 cups milk
- 1 1/2 cups sharp cheddar cheese
- 1/2 cup Gruyère cheese
- 1/2 tsp paprika
- 1/2 cup panko breadcrumbs

Instructions:

1. Cook macaroni, drain.
2. Make a roux with butter and flour, then whisk in milk.
3. Stir in cheeses and paprika.
4. Fold in pasta and lobster.
5. Top with breadcrumbs and bake at 375°F (190°C) for 15 minutes.

Thai Spicy Prawn Tom Yum Soup

Ingredients:

- 1/2 lb shrimp
- 4 cups chicken broth
- 2 lemongrass stalks, chopped
- 3 kaffir lime leaves
- 2 garlic cloves, minced
- 1 tbsp Thai chili paste
- 1 tbsp fish sauce
- 1/2 cup mushrooms
- Juice of 1 lime

Instructions:

1. Simmer broth with lemongrass, lime leaves, garlic, and chili paste.
2. Add mushrooms, fish sauce, and shrimp. Cook until shrimp turns pink.
3. Finish with lime juice.

Truffle-Infused Lobster Risotto

Ingredients:

- 1 lobster tail, cooked and chopped
- 1 cup Arborio rice
- 3 cups seafood broth
- 1/4 cup white wine
- 1/2 onion, finely chopped
- 1 tbsp butter
- 1 tbsp truffle oil
- 1/4 cup Parmesan cheese

Instructions:

1. Heat broth.
2. Sauté onion in butter, add Arborio rice.
3. Stir in wine, cook until absorbed.
4. Gradually add broth, stirring until creamy.
5. Stir in Parmesan, truffle oil, and lobster.

Charred Mackerel with Pickled Vegetables

Ingredients:

- 2 whole mackerel, cleaned and filleted
- 1 tbsp olive oil
- 1 tsp sea salt
- 1/2 tsp black pepper
- 1/2 tsp smoked paprika

For Pickled Vegetables:

- 1/2 cup rice vinegar
- 1 tbsp sugar
- 1 tsp salt
- 1 carrot, julienned
- 1 cucumber, julienned
- 1/2 red onion, thinly sliced

Instructions:

1. Mix vinegar, sugar, and salt. Add vegetables and let sit for 20 minutes.
2. Heat a grill pan. Rub mackerel with olive oil, salt, pepper, and paprika.
3. Sear skin-side down for 3-4 minutes until charred. Flip and cook 1-2 more minutes.
4. Serve with pickled vegetables.

Fried Soft-Shell Crab with Remoulade

Ingredients:

- 4 soft-shell crabs, cleaned
- 1 cup buttermilk
- 1 cup cornmeal
- 1/2 cup flour
- 1 tsp Old Bay seasoning
- 1/2 tsp salt
- Vegetable oil for frying

For Remoulade:

- 1/2 cup mayonnaise
- 1 tbsp Dijon mustard
- 1 tbsp capers, chopped
- 1 tbsp relish
- 1 tsp hot sauce
- 1 tsp lemon juice

Instructions:

1. Soak crabs in buttermilk for 10 minutes.
2. Mix cornmeal, flour, Old Bay, and salt. Dredge crabs in mixture.
3. Heat oil to 350°F (175°C) and fry crabs for 2-3 minutes per side.
4. Mix remoulade ingredients and serve with crabs.

Szechuan-Style Spicy Lobster

Ingredients:

- 2 lobster tails, chopped
- 1 tbsp Szechuan peppercorns
- 2 tbsp soy sauce
- 1 tbsp chili paste
- 1 tbsp ginger, minced
- 2 garlic cloves, minced
- 2 green onions, chopped
- 1 tbsp sesame oil

Instructions:

1. Heat sesame oil, fry peppercorns for 30 seconds.
2. Add garlic, ginger, and chili paste. Stir-fry for 1 minute.
3. Add lobster, soy sauce, and cook until opaque.
4. Garnish with green onions.

Butter-Basted Grouper Fillet

Ingredients:

- 2 grouper fillets
- 2 tbsp butter
- 1 tbsp olive oil
- 2 garlic cloves, smashed
- 1 sprig thyme
- Salt & pepper

Instructions:

1. Heat oil in a pan. Season fillets with salt and pepper.
2. Sear for 3-4 minutes. Add butter, garlic, and thyme.
3. Baste fillets with butter while cooking for another 2 minutes.

Scallop and Saffron Cream Pasta

Ingredients:

- 6 large scallops
- 8 oz linguine
- 1/4 cup white wine
- 1/2 cup heavy cream
- 1/4 tsp saffron threads
- 2 tbsp butter
- 2 garlic cloves, minced

Instructions:

1. Cook pasta.
2. Sear scallops in butter for 2 minutes per side. Remove.
3. Add garlic and wine to pan. Simmer.
4. Add saffron and cream, reduce slightly. Toss with pasta and top with scallops.

Smoked Haddock Chowder

Ingredients:

- 1 lb smoked haddock
- 2 cups fish stock
- 1 cup milk
- 1/2 cup heavy cream
- 1 onion, chopped
- 1 potato, diced
- 2 tbsp butter
- 1/2 tsp thyme

Instructions:

1. Sauté onion in butter.
2. Add stock, milk, potatoes, and thyme. Simmer until potatoes soften.
3. Add haddock and cook for 5 minutes. Stir in cream.

Cured Gravlax with Dill Mustard Sauce

Ingredients:

- 1 lb fresh salmon
- 2 tbsp salt
- 1 tbsp sugar
- 1 tbsp black pepper
- 1 bunch dill, chopped
- 1 tbsp lemon zest

For Sauce:

- 1/4 cup Dijon mustard
- 1 tbsp honey
- 1 tbsp chopped dill
- 1 tbsp lemon juice

Instructions:

1. Rub salmon with salt, sugar, pepper, dill, and zest. Wrap tightly and refrigerate for 24-48 hours.
2. Rinse, slice thinly. Mix sauce ingredients and serve.

Spanish Gambas al Ajillo (Garlic Shrimp)

Ingredients:

- 1/2 lb shrimp, peeled
- 4 garlic cloves, sliced
- 2 tbsp olive oil
- 1/2 tsp red pepper flakes
- 1 tbsp lemon juice
- 1 tbsp chopped parsley

Instructions:

1. Heat oil, sauté garlic until golden.
2. Add shrimp and red pepper flakes. Cook for 2-3 minutes.
3. Finish with lemon juice and parsley.

Teriyaki-Glazed Yellowtail

Ingredients:

- 2 yellowtail fillets
- 1/4 cup soy sauce
- 2 tbsp mirin
- 1 tbsp honey
- 1 tsp ginger, grated

Instructions:

1. Mix soy sauce, mirin, honey, and ginger.
2. Marinate fish for 30 minutes.
3. Sear fillets in a hot pan for 3-4 minutes per side.

Baked Clams Casino

Ingredients:

- 12 littleneck clams
- 4 strips bacon, chopped
- 1/4 cup breadcrumbs
- 1 tbsp butter
- 1 garlic clove, minced
- 1 tbsp parsley, chopped
- 1 tbsp Parmesan cheese

Instructions:

1. Preheat oven to 375°F (190°C).
2. Sauté bacon until crispy, then add garlic.
3. Mix bacon, breadcrumbs, butter, parsley, and cheese.
4. Spoon onto clams and bake for 12 minutes.

Japanese Uni (Sea Urchin) Sashimi

Ingredients:

- 4 fresh uni (sea urchin) trays
- 1 sheet shiso leaf (optional)
- 1 tbsp soy sauce
- 1 tsp wasabi
- 1 tbsp ponzu sauce

Instructions:

1. Arrange uni on a plate with shiso leaf.
2. Serve with soy sauce, ponzu, and wasabi on the side.
3. Enjoy fresh, without overpowering flavors.

Mediterranean Stuffed Squid

Ingredients:

- 4 whole squid, cleaned
- 1/2 cup cooked rice
- 1/4 cup feta cheese, crumbled
- 1/4 cup sun-dried tomatoes, chopped
- 1/2 tsp oregano
- 2 garlic cloves, minced
- 2 tbsp olive oil
- 1/2 cup white wine

Instructions:

1. Mix rice, feta, tomatoes, oregano, and garlic. Stuff into squid.
2. Heat olive oil in a pan, sear squid for 2 minutes per side.
3. Add white wine and simmer for 5 minutes. Serve warm.

Cajun Blackened Redfish

Ingredients:

- 2 redfish fillets
- 2 tbsp Cajun seasoning
- 1 tbsp butter
- 1 tbsp olive oil
- Lemon wedges

Instructions:

1. Rub Cajun seasoning on fillets.
2. Heat butter and oil in a pan.
3. Sear fish for 3-4 minutes per side until blackened.
4. Serve with lemon wedges.

New England Lobster Roll

Ingredients:

- 2 lobster tails, cooked and chopped
- 2 tbsp mayonnaise
- 1 tsp lemon juice
- 1 tbsp chives, chopped
- 2 brioche buns
- 1 tbsp butter

Instructions:

1. Mix lobster, mayo, lemon juice, and chives.
2. Butter and toast brioche buns.
3. Fill buns with lobster mixture.

Hokkaido Scallop Carpaccio

Ingredients:

- 6 Hokkaido scallops, thinly sliced
- 1 tbsp olive oil
- 1/2 tsp sea salt
- 1 tsp yuzu juice
- 1/2 tsp black pepper
- 1 tsp tobiko (fish roe)

Instructions:

1. Arrange scallop slices on a plate.
2. Drizzle with olive oil, yuzu, and season with salt and pepper.
3. Garnish with tobiko.

Icelandic Salted Cod with Potatoes

Ingredients:

- 1 lb salted cod, soaked overnight
- 4 potatoes, boiled and sliced
- 1 onion, sliced
- 2 tbsp butter
- 1 tbsp parsley, chopped

Instructions:

1. Sauté onions in butter until caramelized.
2. Boil cod until flaky.
3. Serve cod with potatoes, onions, and parsley.

Sicilian-Style Grilled Sardines

Ingredients:

- 8 fresh sardines, cleaned
- 2 tbsp olive oil
- 1 tsp sea salt
- 1/2 tsp red pepper flakes
- 1 tbsp lemon juice
- 1 tbsp parsley

Instructions:

1. Brush sardines with olive oil and season with salt and pepper.
2. Grill for 2-3 minutes per side.
3. Finish with lemon juice and parsley.

Alaskan Spot Prawns with Garlic Butter

Ingredients:

- 6 Alaskan spot prawns, peeled
- 3 tbsp butter
- 2 garlic cloves, minced
- 1 tbsp lemon juice
- 1 tbsp parsley, chopped

Instructions:

1. Melt butter, add garlic, and sauté for 1 minute.
2. Add prawns and cook for 2 minutes per side.
3. Finish with lemon juice and parsley.

Poached Monkfish in Saffron Broth

Ingredients:

- 2 monkfish fillets
- 2 cups fish stock
- 1/4 tsp saffron threads
- 1/2 cup white wine
- 1 shallot, minced
- 1 tbsp butter

Instructions:

1. Heat butter, sauté shallot, then add saffron, wine, and stock.
2. Simmer monkfish in broth for 10 minutes.
3. Serve with broth drizzled over.

Seaweed-Wrapped Grilled Eel (Unagi)

Ingredients:

- 2 fillets unagi (eel)
- 1 sheet nori (seaweed)
- 1 tbsp eel sauce
- 1 tbsp soy sauce

Instructions:

1. Brush eel with eel sauce and grill for 3 minutes per side.
2. Cut into pieces and wrap with nori.

Italian Frutti di Mare (Seafood Pasta)

Ingredients:

- 8 oz spaghetti
- 1/2 lb mixed seafood (shrimp, mussels, calamari)
- 2 garlic cloves, minced
- 1/4 tsp red pepper flakes
- 1/2 cup white wine
- 1/2 cup tomato sauce
- 2 tbsp olive oil

Instructions:

1. Cook spaghetti.
2. Heat olive oil, sauté garlic and red pepper flakes.
3. Add seafood, cook for 3 minutes.
4. Pour in wine and tomato sauce. Simmer for 5 minutes.
5. Toss with pasta and serve.

www.ingramcontent.com/pod-product-compliance
Lightning Source LLC
LaVergne TN
LVHW081500060526
838201LV00056BA/2860